GROUNDCOVER
SERIES

Text research: David McDonald and Chris Carr for Curran Publishing Services

To my parents, Lynwen and Arnold

Acknowledgements

I would like to thank a number of people who have helped me
during the preparation of this book.

First and foremost, my wife Delyth and family for all their encouragement
and support. Special thanks go to Christopher Robinson and the staff at
Canterbury Cathedral; Ruth Wood at Leeds Castle; Amanda Harris-Deans at
Higham Park; Bonnie Vernon; English Heritage; The National Trust; the staff
of Imperial college at Wye and the staff at Minster Abbey. Photographs
of Penshurst Place are by kind permission of Viscount De L'Isle. Photographs
on pages 12–17 are by kind permission of The Dean and Chapter of
Canterbury Cathedral.

I particularly wish to thank Sarah Letts for her continued help and advice,
along with Kaarin Wall, Malcolm Crampton and everyone at Jarrold.

Geraint Tellem

Front cover picture: Chirst Church Gate, Canterbury
Back cover picture: North Downs near Thurnham

Designed and produced by
Jarrold Publishing,
Whitefriars, Norwich NR3 1TR

All photographs
© Geraint Tellem
The image on page 24 is
reproduced by kind
permission of Klaus Ringwald.

© Jarrold Publishing 2002

ISBN 0-7117-2079-7

Printed in Belgium.

1/02

PUBLISHER'S NOTE
Variant and archaic spellings have
been retained in quoted material,
while the modern spellings of
place-names have been used in
headings.
  The inclusion of a photograph
in this book does not necessarily
imply public access to the building
illustrated.

CANTERBURY AND KENT

Geraint Tellem

JARROLD publishing

Copper Kettle Tea Rooms, Chilham

CANTERBURY AND KENT

GROUNDCOVER
SERIES

Hay bale, near Wingham

Contents

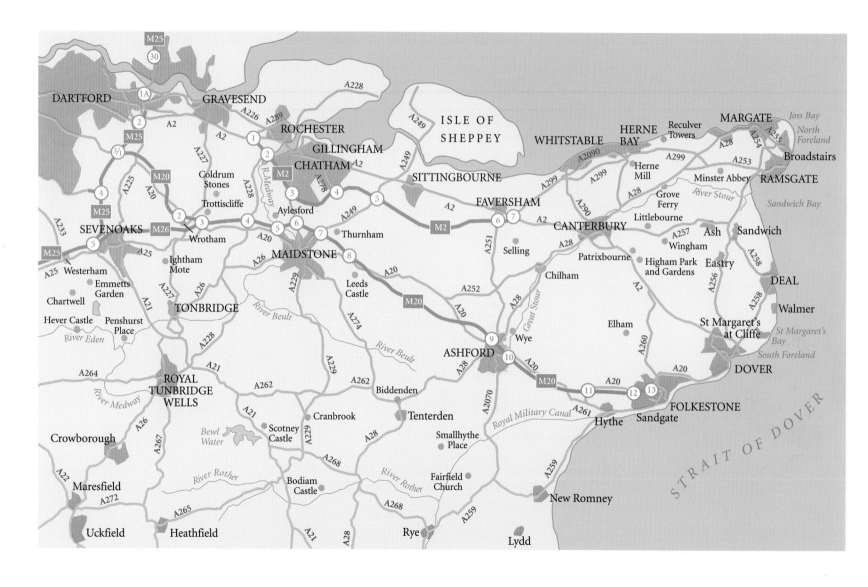

Introduction

Viewed from a distance, there can be no doubt that Canterbury is dominated by the glorious majesty of its cathedral. The first glimpse of its towers and spires has welcomed the thousands of pilgrims who have flocked to the city over the centuries.

Canterbury originally developed as a strategic settlement on the banks of the Stour, with Belgic tribes settling here as early as 33BC. The Romans established a town by the name of Durovernum after their arrival in 43AD but during the 6th century this was renamed Cantwarabyrig, 'the township of the men of Kent'.

It was the influence of St Augustine, sent by Pope Gregory in AD597 to reconvert England, that led to Canterbury's emergence as one of the great religious centres of the country. His Saxon cathedral was burned down in 1067, but within ten years Archbishop Lanfranc had constructed a replacement, the foundations of which remain to the present day. Numerous masters subsequently added to these, creating what must surely be one of the greatest cathedrals in the world. The brutal murder of Thomas Becket in 1170 precipitated the ascent of Canterbury Cathedral to the most popular place of pilgrimage in Christendom.

Within the walled city, quaint medieval streets coexist with modern development and this juxtaposition of old and new gives the city its unique and distinctive character.

Often referred to as the 'Garden of England', Kent is a county of contrasts. Chalk downland gives way to flat expanses of marsh land; white cliffs merge with wide sandy bays; orchards and hop gardens intermingle with more familiar forms of agriculture. Castles, stately homes and picturesque villages can be found throughout the county but it is the oast house, with its distinctive conical roof and white cowl, which most symbolises Kent. The countryside is typically English in many ways, yet it is easy to forget that in some places mainland Europe is less than twenty-five miles away – on a clear day, the coast of France is easily visible from the cliffs of Dover.

The photographs in this book explore the magnificence of Canterbury and its cathedral before examining the contrasting elements of this south eastern extremity of the country. Whilst great changes are occurring in many areas, there are places where a sense of timelessness still exists, such as in the peaceful Elham valley, or high on the escarpment of the North Downs. Producing the following photographs has been a rewarding experience and I discovered many new and interesting places along the way.

GERAINT TELLEM

WEST FRONT
CANTERBURY
CATHEDRAL

I seemed to be sustained and
led on by my fanciful picture
of my mother in her youth,
before I came into the world.
It always kept me company.
It was there, among the hops,
when I lay down to sleep; it
was with me on my waking in
the morning; it went before
me all day. I have associated
it, ever since, with the sunny
street of Canterbury, dozing
as it were in the hot light; and
with the sight of its old houses
and gateways, and the stately,
grey Cathedral, with the rooks
sailing round the towers.

CHARLES DICKENS
David Copperfield
1850

CANTERBURY
CATHEDRAL

They saw at Canterbury the
    cathedral;
Black Edward's helm, and
    Beckett's bloody stone,
Were pointed out as usual
    by the bedral,
In the same quaint
    uninteresting tone:–
There's glory again for you,
    gentle reader! All
Ends in a rusty casque and
    dubious bone,
Half solved into these sodas
    and magnesias,
Which form that bitter
    draught, the human
    species.

LORD BYRON
*Don Juan's Journey from Dover to
London*
1821

CANTERBURY CATHEDRAL

… all armed in steel for battle, with our arms quartered; and my visage with my helmet of the leopard put under the head.

Directions in the Black Prince's will about his effigy in the nave 1376

ST MICHAEL'S CHAPEL
CANTERBURY CATHEDRAL

Before the Reformation and the complete sweeping away of the enrichments of Roman Catholic times the roof and walls were brilliant with paintings, the windows glowed with the warm colour of medieval glass, sumptuous hangings were suspended in many places and the altars twinkling with lighted candles added much gilding and colour to the aisles. All this … has passed away, but the vast building remains to tell of the reality of endeavour of one side on monastic life.

GORDON HOME
Canterbury
1911

CANTERBURY CATHEDRAL

And specially from every
shires ende
Of Englande to Caunterbury
they wende,
The hooly blisful martir for
to seke,
That hem hath holpen whan
that they were seeke.

GEOFFREY CHAUCER
General Prologue to *The Canterbury Tales*
1386-1400

CANTERBURY CATHEDRAL

Ascending some more steps, the
modern pilgrim reaches Trinity
Chapel, where his eyes, instead of
falling upon a shrine encrusted
with jewels and precious metals,
merely look between the pillars
upon an empty space…By going
closer and examining the
pavement, a shallow groove
appears marking the exact
position of the base of the shrine.
This was worn by the endless
stream of pilgrims as they knelt in
ecstasy before the object their
eyes had longed to feast upon.

GORDON HOME
Canterbury
1911

ST AUGUSTINE'S ABBEY
CANTERBURY

A century ago, when appreciation of the architecture of the dead centuries when Englishmen built with superlative skill had sunk to its lowest, the Abbey had sunk to inconceivably debased uses. The monastic kitchen had been converted into a public house, and the great gateway – the finest structural relic of the Abbey – had become the entrance to a brewery, while cock-fighting took place in the state bedroom above. The pilgrims' guest hall, now the college dining hall, had become a dancing hall.

GORDON HOME
Canterbury
1911

ST AUGUSTINE'S ABBEY
CANTERBURY

In the 1070s 'Canterbury remained, like Caesar's Gaul, divided into three parts – one the property of the see, the second belonging to the Abbey of St Augustine, and the third nominally belonging to the king.'

E. F. LINCOLN
The Story of Canterbury
1955

The Domesday Book values the lands of the cathedral and St Augustine's at nearly half of all Kent. St Augustine's held 29 manors in East Kent alone.

WAR MEMORIAL GARDENS
CANTERBURY

Many men of the volunteer Canterbury Regiment, along with other Kentish soldiers, died in the three Battles of Ypres during the First World War. The town of Ypres itself was devastated, and the destruction of its great medieval cloth hall became a symbol of the war's devastation. After the war, it was decided that the hall should be rebuilt just as it had been, and the work was finally concluded in the 1960s. A stone from the hall presented to Canterbury's Memorial Garden commemorates the mutual tragedy of the two cities.

CANTERBURY

…we came to Canterbury, where as it was market-day my aunt had a great opportunity of insinuating the grey pony among carts, baskets, vegetables and hucksters' goods. The hair-breadth turns and twists we made, drew upon us a variety of speeches from the people standing about, which were not always complementary; but my aunt drove with perfect indifference…

CHARLES DICKENS
David Copperfield
1850

CHRIST CHURCH GATE
CANTERBURY

Canterbury suffered greatly during the Civil War. Parliament's soldiers pulled down the carved oak gates, and they were not replaced until the restoration of the King in 1660. They also damaged the statue of Christ that stood above the gates, the statue was dragged down and smashed to pieces. The niche stood empty for 350 years until the statue of Christ Blessing by Klaus Ringwald was installed in 1992.

CHRIST CHURCH GATE
CANTERBURY

The gates were built by Henry VII, probably in memory of his oldest son Arthur, who died at the age of 16. In the centre is Henry's coat of arms, the leopards of England and the lillies of France, supported by the Welsh dragon. Beside it is the Tudor rose, and the arms of Catherine of Aragon, Arthur's wife, who was later the first wife of Henry VIII.

CANTERBURY

That toward Caunterbury wolden ryde.

The chambres and the stables weren wyde,

And wel we weren esed atte beste.

And shortly, whan the sonne was to reste…

GEOFFREY CHAUCER
General Prologue to *The Canterbury Tales*
1386-1400

THOMAS BECKET INN
CANTERBURY

I believe I could make it out, that a poor labouring man may live as cheap in Kent or Sussex as in the bishoprick of Durham; and yet in Kent a poor man shall earn 7s. 10s. 9s. a week, and in the north 4s. or perhaps less; the difference is plain in this, that in Kent there is a greater want of people, in proportion to the work there, than in the north.

DANIEL DEFOE
Giving Alms No Charity
1704

ROYAL MUSEUM
CANTERBURY

James Beaney, son of a labourer, was helped by local philanthropists to study medicine in Edinburgh. After serving as a surgeon in the army and navy, and failing in business as a chemist, he set out for the goldrush in Australia in 1857. By the 1890s his ostentation, high earnings and books on venereal disease had earned him the nickname 'Diamond Jimmy'. On his death he left £10,000 for an institute 'for the education of the Labouring Man'. He also left £1,000 for his memorial, to be seen in the Cathedral nave.

ROYAL MUSEUM
AND
FREE LIBRARY.
(FOUNDED 1858)

CANTERBURY CASTLE

The castle conforms with the other medieval buildings of Canterbury in that it is very obviously composed in part of Roman materials. There are the tell-tale thin red Roman bricks haphazardly placed in the fabric as well as a good deal of other material which with equal certainty, though less obviously, is attributed to Roman times.

E. F. LINCOLN
The Story of Canterbury
1955

CONQUEST HOUSE
CANTERBURY

VANGUARD of Liberty, ye men of Kent,
Ye children of a Soil that doth advance
Her haughty brow against the coast of France,
Now is the time to prove your hardiment!
To France be words of invitation sent!
They from their fields can see the
    countenance
Of your fierce war, may ken the glittering
    lance
And hear you shouting forth your brave
    intent.
Left single, in bold parley, ye, of yore,
Did from the Norman win a gallant wreath…
Confirmed the charters that were yours
    before;
No parleying now! In Britain is one breath;
We all are with you now from shore to shore:–
Ye men of Kent, 'tis victory or death!

WILLIAM WORDSWORTH
To the Men of Kent
1803

WEST GATE GROVE
CANTERBURY

This maketh me at home
    to hunt and hawk
And in foul weather at my
    book to sit.
In frost and snow then
    with my bow to stalk
No man doth mark where
    I so ride or go;
In lusty lees my liberty
    I take…
Here I am in Kent and
    Christendome,
Among the muses where
    I read and rhyme.

THOMAS WYATT THE ELDER
Mine Own John Poynz
1557

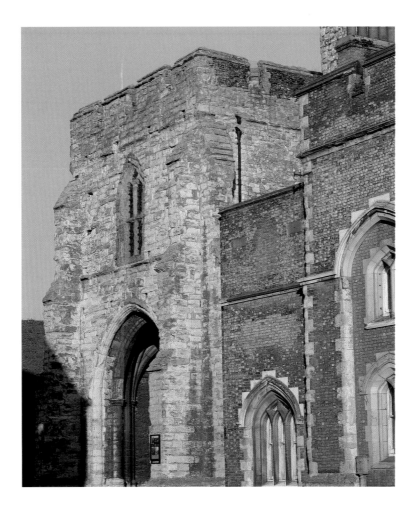

WEST GATE
CANTERBURY

The key-hole shaped loopholes on West Gate are designed for cannon, and this was perhaps the first fortification defended by guns in England. It was erected by Archbishop Simon Sudbury, who was executed in the Peasants' Revolt of 1381 and whose headless body is buried in the cathedral. John Leland, the sixteenth-century English antiquary, called Sudbury 'a great repairer of the city'.

DANE JOHN GARDENS
CANTERBURY

In 1539 Dr John Stone, a friar of Canterbury, was martyred at the Dane John for denying that Henry VIII was head of the Church. In prison 'after an uninterrupted fast of three days, he heard a voice, but without seeing the presence of anyone, calling him by name and exhorting him to be of good courage and not to hesitate to suffer with constancy for the truth of the opinion which he had professed'.

R. A. STANTON
Menology of England and Wales
1887

DANE JOHN BURIAL MOUND AND ARTHUR SIMMONS MEMORIAL
CANTERBURY

After 1066, the Normans threw up wooden castles to hold down their conquest. One of the first was at Canterbury, built on a massive earthwork raised over an Iron Age burial mound. The name Dane John comes from the Norman 'donjon' (castle mound).

DANE JOHN GARDENS
CANTERBURY

A prominent citizen, Alderman Simmons, provided the funds to lay out the Dane John Gardens as they are today. One may say that Alderman Simmons' enthusiasm was greater than his knowledge or taste, for the work he sponsored included the remodelling of Dane John itself and the erection of a memorial on its summit. Yet … the result was a magnificent addition to the amenities of eighteenth-century Canterbury.

E. F. LINCOLN
The Story of Canterbury
1955

MARLOWE THEATRE
CANTERBURY

Christopher Marlowe was baptised in St George's Church at the other end of the city (only the clock tower survives). He may well have had the West Gate of his native city in mind when he wrote in *The Jew of Malta*: 'Two lofty towers that command the town, I wonder how it could be conquered thus.'

SIR JOHN BOYS' HOUSE
CANTERBURY

With its famous leaning doorway, due to a chimney alteration, Sir John Boys' House is one of the most photographed houses in England.

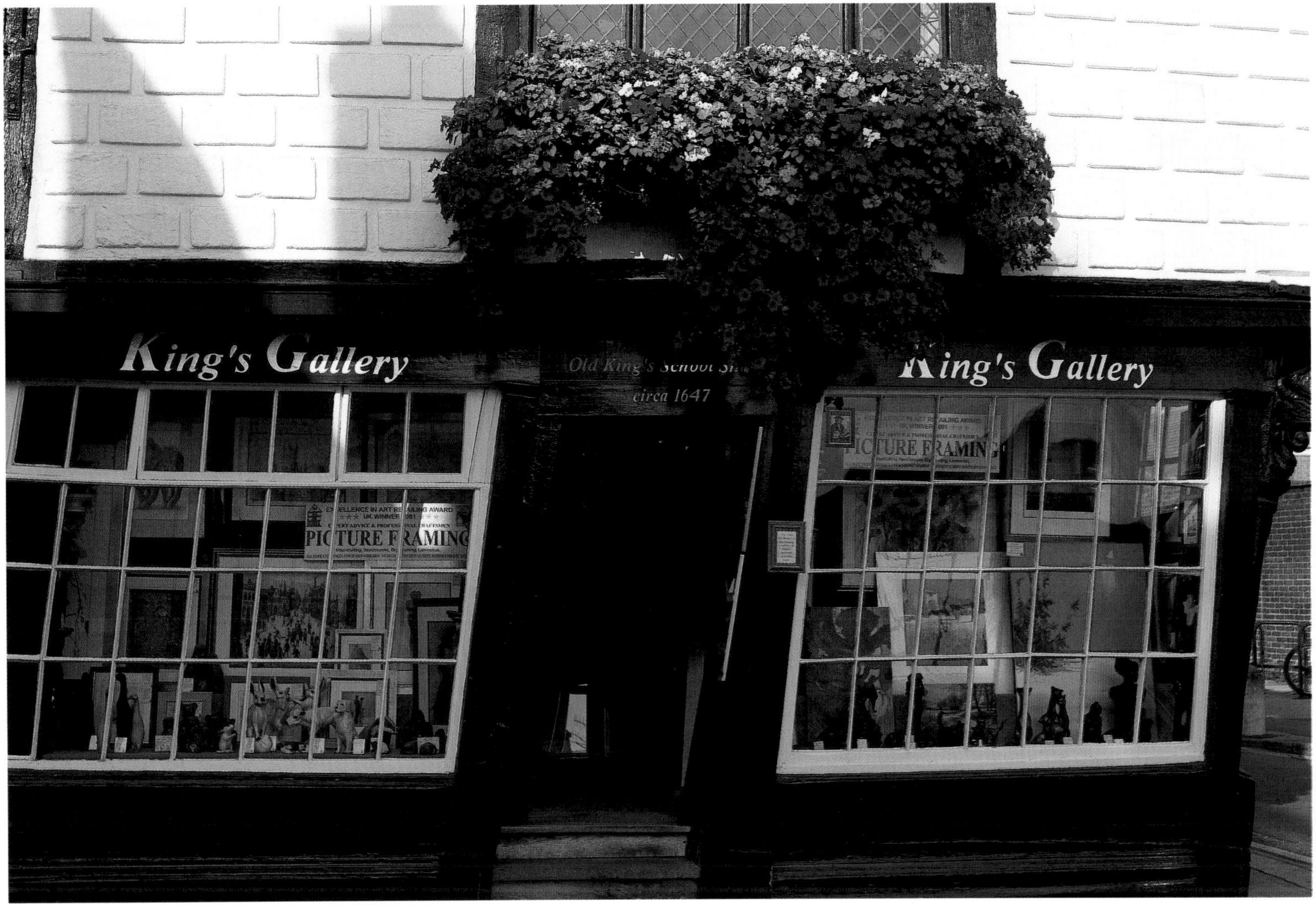
King's Gallery
circa 1647
King's Gallery
PICTURE FRAMING

The Old Weavers House
A.D. 1500
The Old Weavers' house A.D.1500
HISTORIC BUILDING OF KENT
The Weavers
Restaurant
River Tours
Old Weavers House A.D.1500.

THE OLD WEAVERS' HOUSE
Canterbury

Overlooking the King's Bridge, The Old Weavers' House stands on a former twelfth-century hall-house, the structure of which still survives under later fabrics.

ST MARTIN'S CHURCH
Canterbury

St Martin's Church, built in Roman times, has been in use since it was restored in the sixth century by Queen Bertha of Kent, and is said to be the oldest parish church still in use in England. Roman brickwork can still be seen in its walls.

HAY BALES
WINGHAM

It should be more people brought over from foreign parts. I do not mean that those we have should be taken from all common employments and put to our manufacture; we may unequally dispose of our hands, and so have too many for some works, and too few for others; and 'tis plain that in some parts of England it is so, what else can be the reason, why in our southern parts of England, Kent in particular, borrows 20,000 people of other counties to get in her harvest.

DANIEL DEFOE
Giving Alms No Charity
1704

ELHAM

Anciently a market town Elham
…has given its name to a
beautiful valley which breaks
through the chalk here in a
southerly direction to Folkestone,
and northerly at the western foot
of the Barham Downs towards
Canterbury.

WALTER JERROLD
Highways and Byways in Kent
1907

CHILHAM

…Thence we come to Chilham, or, as some call it, Julham, where are the ruins of an old castle, which one Fulbert de Dover is said to have built…The current tradition among the people here is that Julius Cæsar incamped here in his second expedition against the Britons, and that thence it was called Julham or Julius's Station…Below this town is a tumulus covered with green turf, under which they say was buried many ages since one Jullaber, whom some fancy a giant, others a witch.

WILLIAM CAMDEN
Camden's Britannia
1586

HOPS

Remember thy hop-yard,
    if season be dry,
Now dig it and weed it
    and so let it lie.
More fenny the layer,
    the better his lust,
More apt to bear hops when
    it crumbles like dust.

THOMAS TUSSER
*Five hundred points of good
husbandry*
1557

HOP GARDEN NEAR BEKESBOURNE

Beere, is a Dutch boorish liquor, a thing not known in England, till of late days an Alien to our Nation, till such times as Hops and Heresies came against us, it is a saucy intruder in this land…And now in late days it is much used in England to the detriment of many Englishmen…for the drink, is a cold drink; yet it doth make a man fat and doth inflate the belly…

ANDREW BOORDE
Dyettary
1545

RECULVER TOWERS

The sister towers of Reculver are a familiar landmark between London and Margate. In ancient times Reculver, under its Roman name of Regulbium, guarded the north entrance to the channel of the Wantsume as did Richborough the south. Lying somewhat out of the direct line, it is not referred to by Latin writers so frequently as the other fort, although recent excavations indicate that Reculver was built as a stone walled fort before Richborough was given walls.

WARD LOCK'S RED GUIDE
The Kent Coast
1965

RECULVER TOWERS

Proceeding along an open shore abounding with shell fish and oysters and plenty of oyster-pits, we come to Reculver, called by the Saxons 'Reaculf'… Ethelbert, king of Kent, after he had given Canterbury to Austin… At present it is only a small country village, and owes all of its consequences to that monastery, whose church spires are of use to mariners to avoid the shoals and sands in the Thames' mouth.

WILLIAM CAMDEN
Camden's Britannia
1586

GROVE FERRY

The pleasantest route to Grove Ferry, which lies a little south of the main road, on the River Stour, is by the footpath at the farther side of the inn. This drops gently through meadows to the river…Grove Ferry, once famous for its lavender plantations, is a noted fishing centre and a popular place for picnics…

WARD LOCK'S RED GUIDE
The Kent Coast
1965

HERNE MILL

A mill has stood here since the sixteenth century. It continued to work as a windmill until 1980, and is still in working order with much of the original machinery.

RIVER STOUR

Centuries of draining
and flood control have
tamed the Stour, that
once kept this region a
natural wetland. In
spring and summer,
migrants include reed
and sedge warblers
and another rarity,
the bearded tit.

ST MARY'S CHURCH
PATRIXBOURNE

The elaborate doorway,
one of the finest in Kent,
was probably built by the
same masons who worked
on nearby Barfreston
Church and Rochester
Cathedral. Christ sits in
the centre, surrounded by
apocalyptic creatures and
angels, carved with
extraordinary detail.

HIGHAM PARK

This Palladian mansion served in the war years as home to Charles de Gaulle. Abandoned for many years, the house and the suberb landscaped gardens, created in the fourteenth century, have been uncovered and extensively restored, along with an Italian water garden and sunken rose terrace. A previous occupant was Countess Zborowski who, with her son Louis, developed the original 'Chitty Chitty Bang Bang' racing cars.

BUCKWELL
OAST HOUSE
Near Canterbury

Kent, sir – everybody knows Kent –
apples, cherries, hops and women.

Charles Dickens
The Pickwick Papers
1836–7

BLEAK HOUSE
Broadstairs

Bleak House (formerly Fort House) was
built during the Napoleonic wars as a
residence for the captain of the Fort.
Both Wilkie Collins and Charles
Dickens lived here, and it is where
Dickens wrote much of *David
Copperfield* as well as other novels. A
later owner converted the house into its
present castellated shape and renamed
it 'Bleak House', claiming Dickens had
used it as the model for his novel of the
same name (though in fact the house in
the novel was located in Hertfordshire).

BROADSTAIRS

The ocean lies winking in the sunlight like a drowsy lion; its glassy waters scarcely curve upon the shore; the fishing boats in the busy harbour are all stranded in the mud. Our two colliers…have not an inch of quarter within a quarter of a mile of them and turn exhausted on their sides, like faint fish of an antediluvian species…The tide has risen; the boats are dancing on the bubbling water; the colliers are afloat again; the white bordered waves rush in…The radiant sails are gliding past the shore and shining on the far horizon; all the sea is sparkling; heaving swelling up with life and beauty this bright morning.

CHARLES DICKENS
From 'Our English Watering Place'

1851

RAMSGATE

Ramsgate is justly proud of the part it played in World War II. The Harbour became a front-line naval base as a reserve to Dover, and many of the 'little ships' which sped to the rescue of the Allied troops on Dunkirk beaches set out from Ramsgate Harbour. About one-third of the troops evacuated from Dunkirk were landed at Ramsgate.

WARD LOCK'S RED GUIDE
The Kent Coast
1965

LITTLEBOURNE

It is a delight to stand by the old water-mill, or by the charming green with cottages yellow and red, with gables and dormers, with the white caps of oasthouses peeping over red roofs.

ARTHUR MEE
The King's England: Kent
1936

MINSTER ABBEY
ISLE OF THANET

Minster Abbey was founded in 670AD by Domneva, a Mercian princess, and her daughter, St Mildred, became the second abbess. The third abbess, Eadburgha, was a correspondent of St Boniface. The crypt is still largely Saxon work, while the smoke-stained chestnut roof of the hall shows that it was in use long before chimneys were first developed (around 1320).

JOSS BAY

The smuggler leader Joss Snelling, took his name from this landing site. In 1769 his gang fought the notorious 'Battle of Botany Bay'. He was later presented to Queen Victoria as 'the famous Broadstairs smuggler'.

THE CRISPIN
SANDWICH

The St Crispin Inn is known to have been in existence since medieval times (though documentary evidences goes back only to 1824). Inns of this name were also the official meeting places of shoemakers and workers in leather, of whom St Crispin is the patron saint.

DEAL CASTLE

Built by Henry VIII in 1539–40 to carry 119 guns, Deal Castle still stands by the sea front and is preserved as an ancient monument by English Heritage. Its shape is very different from earlier castles, the low, squat silhouette and tremendously thick walls showing how cannon had changed the architecture of war. Its bastions form the shape of a six-petalled Tudor rose so that it, together with its sister forts at Walmer and Sandown, were known as 'the three roses'.

NORTH FORELAND LIGHTHOUSE

The North Foreland was known to the Romans as Cantium, and is said to have been the site of a lighthouse as far back as 1505, though for many years the light was merely a coal fire.

Ward Lock's Red Guide
The Kent Coast
1965

WALMER CASTLE

Walmer Castle is the official home of the Lord Warden of the Cinque Ports. The Duke of Wellington was once a Warden and lived here for 23 years. It was also home to Australian Prime Minister Sir Robert Menzies on his visits to Britain. The castle was built between 1539 and 1540 as the southernmost of a chain of forts defending the south coast.

WALMER CASTLE

It is the best of the three Tudor roses that Cromwell pulled in 13 days; he took the three castles of Walmer, Deal and Sandown, all built in the shape of a Tudor rose, all standing within three miles, facing the Goodwin sands…We enter the castle through the great oak doors and are glad that we are welcome, for ominous holes in the roof remind us that molten lead was dropped through them from the roof to surprise unwelcome visitors.

ARTHUR MEE
The King's England: Kent
1936

SOUTH FORELAND LIGHTHOUSE

Set on the White Cliffs near St Margaret's-at-Cliffe, the South Foreland Lighthouse was built in 1843. Marconi used it in the earliest wireless experiments, sending the first ship-to-shore signal to the lighthouse in 1898 and, the next year, the first wireless message from France to England. The first SOS signal was received here on 3 March 1899, when a freighter rammed the East Goodwin Lightship. Some years later a similar call was received from the *Titanic*, her crew desperately trying to prevent her sinking after they'd hit an iceberg.

ST MARGARET'S BAY

…no hint of the beauties below is given until the edge of the cliff is reached, when a bird's eye view is obtained of a crescent-shaped, shingly strand, then trees and undergrowth, broken into patches by break-neck paths straggling up the cliff-side; and all over the dazzling glare of the chalk…

WARD LOCK'S RED GUIDE
The Kent Coast
1965

DOVER CASTLE

At sunset the bridge shall be drawn, and the gates shut; afterwards the guard shall be mounted by 20 warders on the castle walls…It is established by ancient rule that if a chief guard discover a warden asleep he shall take something from him as he lies, or carry away his staff, or cut a piece out of part of his clothes, to witness against him in case the warder should deny being asleep, and he shall lose his day's wage…

FROM THE INSTRUCTIONS OF CONSTABLE SIR STEPHEN DE PENCESTRE TO THE GARRISON OF DOVER CASTLE

1267

DOVER PATROL MEMORIAL
ST MARGARET'S BAY

The Dover Patrol was set up to protect shipping from mines and submarine attack during the First World War. On St George's Day 1918 they launched a desperate attack on Zeebrugge to prevent its use as a submarine base. The memorial was erected in 1921, and a remembrance ceremony is held on the anniversary of the Zeebrugge raid, 23 April, each year.

BATTLE OF BRITAIN MEMORIAL (LEFT) AND FOLKESTONE HARBOUR (RIGHT)

The sea is calm to-night.
The tide is full, the moon lies fair
Upon the straits; – on the French coast
    the light
Gleams and is gone; the cliffs of England
    stand,
Glimmering and vast, out in the tranquil bay.
Come to the window, sweet is the night-air!
Only, from the long line of spray
Where the sea meets the moon-
    blanched land,
Listen! you hear the grating roar
Of pebbles which the waves draw back,
    and fling,
At their return, up the high strand,
Begin, and cease, and then again begin,
With tremulous cadence slow, and bring
The eternal note of sadness in.

MATTHEW ARNOLD *New Poems* 1867

CHURCH OF ST MARY THE VIRGIN
Selling

The Church of St Mary the Virgin is noted for its fine bell tower. The profusion of churches in Kent attest its wealth in the Middle Ages; their bells could be heard in every part of the region, and England was known as 'the ringing Isle'.

CHARING

Its street is one long charm, whether we go up the hill towards Canterbury, with its height of over 600 feet, or down the hill towards Ashford. The overhanging houses, the oriel windows, the great canopy over the pavement at the butcher's shop, the lovely almshouses, the wealth of old oak everywhere, the white windmill looking down on it all, the old inns, the narrow passages, and the ruins of ages standing round about, make Charing one of Kent's most charming scenes. It was kind of the great road to go round and leave this place a little quiet.

ARTHUR MEE
The King's England: Kent
1936

IMPERIAL COLLEGE
WYE

The college at Wye was founded in 1447 by Cardinal John Kempe, a native of Wye who became Lord Chancellor and Archbishop successively of York and Canterbury. It began as the 'College of St Gregory and St Martin', a training college for priests and has had a virtually continuous history as a centre of study for about 550 years. It became a college of higher education in 1894, and has been part of London University since 1900. It now has a world-wide reputation as a leading centre of studies in agriculture and countryside management, with students from over 40 different countries.

SMALLHYTHE PLACE

When Smallyhythe Place was built in around 1480, the town was a major shipbuilding centre, using timber from the Wealden forest. Henry V built warships there. The sea has since retreated, but the pond in the garden marks the site of a repair dock that was used for nearly 400 years. Today the house is preserved as a theatrical museum in memory of the great Shakespearean actress Ellen Terry, whose country retreat it was for nearly 30 years.

TENTERDEN

The name Tenterden means 'a swine pasture that belonged to the men of Thanet'. The town flourished in the late fourteenth century on the profits of the wool trade. It was then that the merchants built a magnificent tower for the church, and splendid mansions for themselves, some of which may still be seen.

FAIRFIELD CHURCH

Fairfield is a perfect example of the Marshland churches, set by itself by a water-filled dyke and visible for miles across the flat fields and grassland. Built in the Middle Ages it still has some of the original timbers, but has gone through many cycles of decay and rebuilding. The interior now presents classic eighteenth-century style, with white-painted pews and a black-lined three-decker pulpit.

LEEDS CASTLE
WITH **HENRY VII'S BANQUETING HALL** (RIGHT)

The Domesday Book records that there was a vineyard at Leeds Castle in 1086, one of 40 in the area. The present vineyard is near the site of the one established by Bishop Odo from Bayeaux, half-brother to William the Conqueror. Built by the Normans as a stronghold, it was later rebuilt for comfort and became known as 'Lady's Castle' because of its queenly occupants. These included Eleanor and Margaret, wives of Edward I, Philippa of Hainault, Catherine de Valois (Henry V's 'sweet Kate') and Catherine of Aragon.

QUEEN'S ROOM (LEFT) AND CATHERINE DE VALOIS COAT OF ARMS (RIGHT)
LEEDS CASTLE

King Harry: O Fair Catherine, if you will love me soundly with your French heart, I will be glad to hear you confess it brokenly with your English tongue. Do you like me, Kate?

Catherine: *Pardonnez-moi* I cannot tell vat is 'like me'.

King Harry: An angel is like you, Kate, and you are like an angel.

WILLIAM SHAKESPEARE
Henry V, Act V Scene II
1599

CRANBROOK WINDMILL

Cranbrook Windmill, built in 1814 on the highest point overlooking Cranbrook, measures 72 feet from its base to the top of the cap; it is the tallest windmill in Kent and the second tallest in the British Isles. It has an eight-sided three-storey brick base and a four-storey, fixed wooden tower of white painted weather-board. It has four sails (called sweeps in the Southeast) with patent shutters and a fantail which keeps the sails facing into the wind at all times. Now restored to full working order, it produces flour sold in the mill shop.

NORTH DOWNS
NEAR THURNHAM

Almost the whole county abounds with meadows, pastures and cornfields, is wonderfully fruitful in apples, and also cherries.

WILLIAM CAMDEN
Camden's Britannia
1586

BIDDENDEN

It is the sort of village a museum would like to have. It has a splendid signpost showing the curious Biddenden Maids, and it takes great care of itself as an ancient village should. Centred round its green, a small patch planted with shrubs, its monuments are admirably grouped. Facing each other stand Hendon House and Hendon Hall, both ancient places; the Hall is a farm, the House has a fine old garden and a sundial of 1623. The wrecked windmill, the church tower, with the black-and-white houses, the tithe barn, and the vicar's pond, complete a splendid village group.

ARTHUR MEE
The King's England: Kent
1936

The 'Biddenden Maids', Mary and Eliza, were Siamese twins who lived to the age of 34.

SCOTNEY CASTLE

The castle was named after its founder, Walter de Scotnei, who built it in the thirteenth century. He was afterwards hanged at Winchester for taking too active a part in the royal family squabbles, by poisoning the brother of the Earl of Gloucester, to whom he was steward. The castle was subsequently sold to Chichele, the yeoman Archbishop of Canterbury whose tomb can be seen in the cathedral. It passed from him through his niece to a family named Darrell, who remained Roman Catholic after the dissolution of the monasteries, and therefore had to adopt the expedient of making a secret priest-chamber in the house. It served its purpose in 1598, when the Jesuit Father Blount took refuge here and used the hidden chamber while the queen's officers searched the premises in vain.

RICHARD CHURCH
Kent
1948

IGHTHAM MOTE

The Mote is one of the most, if not the most, perfect moated houses now remaining, the walls rising on all four sides straight out of the water. The house is supposed to have been built in 1180 by Sir Ivo de Haut. Crossing the moat by a stone bridge, and passing through the chief gateway, we enter a courtyard.

DUNCAN MOUL
Week-Ends in Hopland
1900

IGHTHAM MOTE

The name of Ightham is by some said to be derived from the fact of the building standing on an island, therefore meaning the village on the eyot, but other authorities give the name as originally Eightham, or eight boroughs…

Duncan Moul
Week-Ends in Hopland
1900

ELIZABETHAN COTTAGES
Ightham Mote

Ightham Mote is one of the oldest medieval manor houses open to the public in England. It has features from many styles and centuries. Including the chapel with its Tudor painted ceiling, a Jacobean fireplace in the drawing room and eighteenth-century wallpaper.

PENSHURST PLACE

…a view, extending over a pleasant and undulating countryside, was dear to the heart of an eighteenth-century gentleman and the 'prospect' was, as much as anything, the consideration that governed the choice of a site for his house. Knole, Penshurst, Cobham Hall are to be looked at; they are not vantage points from which to admire the view.

F.W. JESSUP
A History of Kent
1995

CHURCH OF ST GEORGE
WROTHAM

The great two-storeyed porch of the church, with an angel in its vaulted roof and a bronze St George at the door, prepares us for its wide interior…The nameless tomb under an arch is said to be that of William de Wrotham, a constable of Dover Castle whose family became extinct 700 years ago – fitting that all these years he should lie in a nameless tomb.

ARTHUR MEE
The King's England: Kent
1936

TONBRIDGE CASTLE

The massive entrance gateway, with its flanking towers, still remains in a good state of preservation. Under the first archway are machicolations for pouring molten lead on any enemy who had succeeded in crossing the fosse to attack the castle. Under the gateway are the dungeons, which are seen through trap doors in the floor. Near the gateway is a huge mound seventy feet high, on top of which formerly stood the keep.

DUNCAN MOUL
Week-Ends in Hopland
1900

NEAR TROTISCLIFFE

The Belgic tribes brought effective ploughing to southern Britain in Caesar's day, and began the transformation of the landscape. To the Saxons who took Kent five centuries later, the word 'field' meant an open space they had cleared from native woodland.

OAST HOUSE
TROTISCLIFFE

Oast houses for drying hops are a distinctive feature of the Kentish countryside. At one time there were over 30,000 acres of hop fields in Kent, and until the 1960s 'foreigners' would come from London for the summer hop-picking.

AYLESFORD

It is a sacred place in the story of our Motherland for here the English established their power. Here they came to stay. Here it was, one day in the year 449 that English history began.

For Aylesford was the first battlefield of the English race. It was here that Hengist and Horsa brought up their forces and fought the ancient Britons… It may be thought that Aylesford's greatest monument is its ancient bridge, the work of the 14th century, with six small arches and a wider central one. One of the noblest monuments of antiquity on the Medway…

ARTHUR MEE
The King's England: Kent
1936

CHURCHILL STATUE
WESTERHAM

Churchill's memorial was unveiled on 23 July 1969 by former Australian Prime Minister Sir Robert Menzies, successor to Churchill as Warden of the Cinque Ports. A public ballot of the people of Westerham had selected the design and site, and virtually the entire population attended the ceremony, together with three generations of the Churchill family. The massive bronze statue by Oscar Nemon stands on a plinth given by 'the people of Yugoslavia'.

CHARTWELL

Chartwell was Winston Churchill's home from 1924 until his death. It is kept still as he left it, with his beloved black swans on the lake and the gardens whose walls he built with his own hands. 'Its roses and azaleas, its araucaria and cedars, and particularly its giant Japanese cedar…tempt one to look out over the Weald expecting to see the Bay of Naples, with Vesuvius smoking in the distance.'

RICHARD CHURCH
Kent
1948

CHARTWELL

The house that Sir Winston Churchill bought was a modest structure. Henry VIII was said to have slept in an oak-panelled room (now gone) in the house, while courting Anne Boleyn at Hever Castle. 'A day away from Chartwell', Churchill once remarked, 'is a day wasted'.

The house is now run by the National Trust, with a number of rooms as he left them, and many of his paintings on display.

HEVER CASTLE

It was at Hever Castle, her childhood home, that Henry VIII courted Anne Boleyn. In 1903, the sadly dilapitated site was bought by the American William Waldorf Astor, who lavished millions of dollars on its restoration, panelling the walls with fine carving and filling the rooms with antiques and tapestries.

APPLES
Near Meopham

Cultivation of apples in England began with the Romans who established colonies of veteran soldiers with plots of land for the growing of fruit. Pliny, in the first century AD, described how farmers would auction the fruit on the trees, a custom still prevalent in Kent 1900 years later. The orchards were abandoned in the Dark Ages, except in monasteries, but revived under the Normans, who introduced new varieties such as the Pearmain and Costard, and also introduced cider making. Half a millennium later, settlers sailing to the new worlds of America and Australia took apple pips with them.

EMMETTS GARDEN

Emmetts Garden displays the passion for botany that was so widespread among the later Victorians. It was laid out in the late nineteenth century under the influence of William Robertson, with many exotic and rare trees and shrubs from across the world, and the highest tree-top in Kent. In spring there are wonderful shows of daffodils and bluebells, with azaleas, rhododendrons, acers and cornus in autumn; there is also a rose garden and rock garden.

EMMETTS GARDEN

The Bluebell is the sweetest
    flower
That waves in summer air:
Its blossoms have the
    mightiest power
To soothe my spirit's care.

ANNE BRONTË
From 'The Bluebell'
1840

QUEEN ELIZABETH II BRIDGE
DARTFORD

At 450 metres long, The Queen Elizabeth II (Dartford) Bridge is Europe's largest cable supported bridge, and is high enough for the tallest liners to pass under the central span. It took three years to build and cost £86 million, raised by eight private companies to be paid back by tolls over a period of 14 to 20 years. It was opened on the 30 October 1991.

COLDRUM LONG BARROW

The best preserved of the Kent megalithic tombs is Coldrum Long Barrow, where the bones of 22 people were found in 1910. It overlooks the Medway valley and has a rectangular burial chamber of four large sarsens at the east end. The upright chamber, partially restored, consists of four large vertical stones on three sides of a rectangle some five feet wide and twelve long.

ROCHESTER CASTLE

I did there walk to visit the old Castle ruines, which hath been a noble place; and there going up, I did upon the stairs overtake three pretty maids or women and took them up with me…but Lord, to see what a dreadful thing it is to look down praecipices, for it did fright me mightily and hinder me of much pleasure which I would have made to myself in the company of these three if it had not been for that.

SAMUEL PEPYS
Diary
2 October 1665

ROCHESTER CATHEDRAL

In Dickens' *The Pickwick Papers* Mr Jingle describes the Cathedral thus: '…Old Cathedral, too – earthy smell – pilgrims' feet worn away the old steps – little Saxon doors – confessionals like money-takers boxes at theatres – queer customs those monks…' In *The Mystery of Edwin Drood* Mr Grewgious looked into the cathedral from the open West Door. 'Dear me' he said, 'it's like looking down the throat of Old Time'.

NORTH DOWNS
NEAR THURNHAM

Kent, in the Commentaries
    Caesar writ,
Is term'd the civil'st place of
    all this isle:
Sweet is the country,
    because full of riches;
The people liberal, valiant,
    active, wealthy,
Which makes me hope you
    are not void of pity.

WILLIAM SHAKESPEARE
Henry IV Part 2, Act IV Scene VII
1598

Apples in orchard, near Chilham

Acknowledgements

Every effort has been made to secure permissions from copyright owners to use the extracts of text featured in this book.

Any subsequent correspondence should be sent to Jarrold Publishing at the following address: Jarrold Publishing, Whitefriars, Norwich NR3 1TR.

page

14 (right) From *Canterbury* (in the Beautiful Britain series) by Gordon Home. Published by Adam & Charles Black. Reproduced by kind permission of A&C Black Publishers Ltd.

17 (right) From *Canterbury* (in the Beautiful Britain series) by Gordon Home. Published by Adam & Charles Black. Reproduced by kind permission of A&C Black Publishers Ltd.

19 (left) From *Canterbury* (in the Beautiful Britain series) by Gordon Home. Published by Adam & Charles Black. Reproduced by kind permission of A&C Black Publishers Ltd.

51 (left) From Ward Lock's Red Guide: *The Kent Coast*. Published by Ward Lock & Co., 1965. Reproduced by kind permission of Cassell & Co.

52 (top) From Ward Lock's Red Guide: *The Kent Coast*. Published by Ward Lock & Co., 1965. Reproduced by kind permission of Cassell & Co.

63 (top) From Ward Lock's Red Guide: *The Kent Coast*. Published by Ward Lock & Co., 1965. Reproduced by kind permission of Cassell & Co.

63 (bottom) *From *The King's England; Kent* by Arthur Mee. First published 1936, Hodder & Stoughton. Reprinted 1939. © The estate of Arthur Mee and The King's England Press Ltd.

69 (bottom) From Ward Lock's Red Guide: *The Kent Coast*. Published by Ward Lock & Co., 1965. Reproduced by kind permission of Cassell & Co.

71 (right)*From *The King's England; Kent* by Arthur Mee. First published 1936, Hodder & Stoughton. Reprinted 1939. © The estate of Arthur Mee and The King's England Press Ltd.

72 (right) From Ward Lock's Red Guide: *The Kent Coast*. Published by Ward Lock & Co., 1965. Reproduced by kind permission of Cassell & Co.

78 (right) *From *The King's England; Kent* by Arthur Mee. First published 1936, Hodder & Stoughton. Reprinted 1939. © The estate of Arthur Mee and The King's England Press Ltd.

93 *From *The King's England; Kent* by Arthur Mee. First published 1936, Hodder & Stoughton. Reprinted 1939. © The estate of Arthur Mee and The King's England Press Ltd.

94 From *Kent* by Richard Church. Published by Robert Hale, 1988. Reproduced by kind permission of Laurence Pollinger Ltd and the Estate of Richard Church.

101 From *A History of Kent* by F. W. Jessup First published by in Phillimore, 1974. Reprinted 1995. Reproduced by kind permission of the publisher.

102 (left) *From *The King's England; Kent* by Arthur Mee. First published 1936, Hodder & Stoughton. Reprinted 1939. © The estate of Arthur Mee and The King's England Press Ltd.

107 (left) *From *The King's England; Kent* by Arthur Mee. First published 1936, Hodder & Stoughton. Reprinted 1939. © The estate of Arthur Mee and The King's England Press Ltd.

108 (left) From *Kent* by Richard Church. Published by Robert Hale, 1988. Reproduced by kind permission of Laurence Pollinger Ltd and the Estate of Richard Church.

116 (top) From *The Shorter Pepys*, edited by Robert Latham. Guild, 1986. Reproduced by kind permission of HarperCollins Publishers Ltd.

*The King's England Press is currently reprinting all of Arthur Mee's King's England county guidebooks in a facsimile edition of the original 1936–1953 editions.

Bibliography

Arnold, Matthew: *New Poems.* Macmillan, 1867.

Barham, Richard Harris: *The Ingoldsby Legends, or Mirth and Madness.* Richard Bentley, 1894.

Bede: *The Ecclesiastical History of*

White Cliffs of Dover at sunset

the English Nation. 8th century. Dent, 1927.

Boorde, Andrew: *Here Foloweth a Compedyous Regyment or a Dyetary of helth, made in Moutpyllor.* Robert Wyer, *c.*1545.

Boyle, John: *The Illustrated Portrait of Canterbury.* First published Robert Hale, 1974. Reprinted 1988.

Byron, Lord: *Don Juan.* First published 1821. John Lane, 1926.

Camden, William: *Camden's Britannia: Kent.* First published 1789. Stockdale 1806.

Church, Richard: *Kent.* Robert Hale, 1948.

Clarendon, Edward Hyde, 1st Earl of: *Selections from The History of the Rebellion and Civil Wars.* First published 1707. Clarendon Press, 1888.

Cobbett, William: *Rural Rides.* London, 1830.

Defoe , Daniel: *A Tour Thorugh the Whole Island of Great Britain 1724—6.* Strahan, 1778.

Defoe, Daniel: 'Giving Alms No Charity' Addressed to the Parliament of England. London: Printed and Sold by the Booksellers of London and Westminster. 1704.

Dickens, Charles: *Great Expectations.* Oxford University Press, 1907.

Dickens, Charles: *The Mystery of Edwin Drood.* First published 1870. Nelson, 1925.

Dickens Charles: *Personal History of David Copperfield.* London Bradbury and Evans 1850.

Dickens, Charles: *Posthumous Papers of the Pickwick Club.* Lawrence & Jellicoe, 1910

Dickens, Charles: 'Our English Watering Place'. *Household Words,* 2 August 1851.

Dickens Charles: *Sketches by Boz.* Macrone, 1837.

Grim, Edward: Vita S. Thomae, Cantuariensis Archepiscopi et Martyris, in James Robertson (ed.) *Materials for the Life of*

Doorway, cottage in Biddenden

Thomas Becket, Volume II. London: Rolls Series, 1875-1885.

Harvey Darton, F. J.: *A Parcel of Kent.* Morrison and Gibb, 1924.

Home, Gordon: *Beautiful Britain: Canterbury.* Adam & Charles Black, 1920.

Jerrold, Walter: *Highways & Byways in Kent.* First published Macmillan, 1907. Reprinted 1923.

Jessup, F. W.: *A History of Kent.* First published Phillimore, 1974. Reprinted 1995.

Jonson, Ben: *The Works of Ben Jonson*, vol. 3., London: Chatto & Windus, 1910.

The Kentish Songster containing above fourteen hundred songs. Third edition, Canterbury 1784.

Lambarde, William: *A Perambulation of Kent* (first published 1576). Baldwin, Cradock and Joy, 1826.

Lincoln, E. F.: *The Story of Canterbury.* Staples, 1955.

Macaulay, Thomas, Lord *History of England.* First published 1855. Everyman 1906.

Maltby, R. and Frankl, E.: *Canterbury.* Pevensey Heritage Guides, 1993.

Mee, Arthur: *The King's England: Kent.* First published 1936, Hodder & Stoughton. Reprinted 1939.

Morris, James: *Pax Britannica.* Faber & Faber, 1968.

Moul, Duncan: *Week-Ends in Hopland.* Homeland Association, 1900.

Nicolson, Nigel: *Kent.* Weidenfeld and Nicolson, 1988.

Pepys, Samuel: *The Shorter Pepys,* edited by Robert Latham. Guild, 1986.

Smart, Christopher: *Poems on Several Occasions.* London, 1752.

Spenser, Edmund: *The Shepheardes Calender – July.* First published 1579. Harper, 1898.

Stanton, R.A.: *Menology of England and Wales.* Burns & Oates, 1887.

Stevenson, Robert Louis: 'The English Admirals'. Cornhill Magazine 38, July 1878. Included in '*Virginibus Puerisque*' and Other Papers. Kegan Paul 1881.

Taylor, John, in. *Miscellanea Antiqua Anglicana*, (Volume III). Hindley, 1871.

Ward Lock's Red Guide: *The Kent Coast.* Ward Lock & Co., 1965.

Winbolt, S. E. and Ward, W.: *Bell's Pocket Guides: Kent.* G. Bell & Sons, 1930.

Wordsworth, William, *The complete poetical works of William Wordsworth.* London & New York: Macmillan & Co., 1888.

Wright, Christopher: *Kent Through the Years.* B. T. Batsford, 1975.

Wyatt, Thomas, *The Poems of Sir Thomas Wiat*, edited by A.K. Foxwell, University of London Press 1913.

Penshurst Place

Elizabethan cottages, Ightham Mote

Index

GROUNDCOVER
SERIES